THEN SPEAKS MY SOUL

Channeled Reflections for Morning Meditation

Azial Starr

To Ray (of sunshine), whose powerful, illuminating light helped me find my way up from the depths.
Also to new life, new beginnings and comets propelled onward by the force of contact with other celestial bodies.

PREFACE

These unedited messages mark my journey of uncovering and accepting my Soul purpose. Each morning on this path of discovery, I would wake and commune with higher frequencies and write down the messages that spontaneously came to me through the voice of my own Soul, or higher self.

I did not edit this version of it, but left the original phrasing to retain the full message. You will find words like Mother, which refer to the Motherly energy of the Earth. You'll also see the word child; to an eternal Soul, our humanity is very child-like in comparison. You'll also read the word God, which refers to the Source energy that resides within us all.

The beginning of the book marks the beginning of my experience of tuning in and accepting messages of love from energy that exists in higher vibrational states. You may find that the unedited passages are rough at first, as I practiced raising my vibrational field to better hear the message and type it out as I heard it. This process is in line with the purpose of the overall message, which is to learn how to tune into the beauty of our eternal Soul and discover our Soul's creation purpose.

Each morning before I begin this process, I would take some time to breathe and be fully present and in a state of absolute love. If this felt difficult, I would write ten things in a gratitude journal that I was grateful for. Gratitude raised my frequency and allowed me to access a higher vibrational state. As time passed, it became easier and easier to access a meditative state of love and beingness. I began to see meditation not as a complicated, drawn out process (which had previously rendered it unattainable), but simply as a sustained state of awareness; a pause from the busyness that life offers to rest in the quietness of being.

This book is not difficult to read or understand, but rather than reading it all at once, I suggest reading a passage upon waking and meditating on the concept presented. This will enable you to maintain the proper outlook for the day and ensure your absolute success in the ultimate process of realization and manifestation.

If you take the time to do this in the morning, even for ten minutes, your whole day will go better.

Also, if you feel like you need an answer to a current dilemma, try flipping through the pages and picking a passage at random for an answer or solution.

Through this daily process of practicing presence and staying in a state of love, came my acceptance, forgiveness and release. I began to understand that love is in actuality an expression of life in its highest vibrational state and the direct path to the most optimal way of living. I was at last to clearly see my life path and am sharing my journey with you in hope that it will help you as well.

Dear One,
The energy that is coming to you now is directly from the Universe.
All of the things you have been dreaming of will come to fruition.
There is synchronicity available for you for the asking.
You are protected by light.
You are being asked to open your heart and mind to more abundance and goodwill.
There is more light and love in store for you this day and there will always be enough.
Say this affirmation aloud now:
I am a divine creature of light capable of achieving my highest calling.
I open now to the abundance which the universe offers.
I stay in alignment with my soul's true purpose which will be revealed to me like the dawning of the morning sun.
There is enough for me.
There is goodness waiting in store for me; I must now let myself receive.

◆ ◆ ◆

You are being asked to clear your mind
Release expectations
Ponder the glorious insignificance of a drop of dew
In the nothing you will find your answers
You are a being of light
Your path is illuminated through small sparks of inspiration
Pay heed to these sparks for they are tinder for the fires of your
soul
A great day is coming in which you will be able to live and express
yourself to your fullest reach
Release your expectations of this day
It is in the stillness that you will find your way
If you quiet your mind, you will see the answer looming before
you
great, powerful and swift results will be yours

Dear One,
There is a difficult concept you must overcome
To achieve a higher state of mind.
There is much beauty in creation
It is for you to see the light in the darkness
You must hold steady, all is not lost
Do not let the misery of the world hold you back from realizing
your potential;
It is not your misery.
You are a being of light
Let go of destructive thought patterns
They will hold you in stasis
There is much joy and progress to be had today
Let the soft light of morning reveal your true purpose
Let the day illuminate your highest calling
There is much in store for you
You must be willing to receive the blessings

◆ ◆ ◆

You are being given a message that brings tidings of a dark period, do not despair.
There is always darkness before there can be great light.
This reality that you have chosen is full of challenges which are being presented to you in accordance with the greater plan.
You must make haste to overcome them and move through the darkness toward the light.

◆ ◆ ◆

Do not let your heart worry.
You have chosen a bumpy road
Learn to ride over it with grace
You must release your fear of abundance,
And be open to receiving it.
Welcome it as an old, dear friend who only has your best interest at heart
There are activities that will distract you from your purpose
Hold steady and do not forget to carry the light
Hold it high and it will illuminate the dark places
Open your heart to receive what is in the making for you
If it comes easily and resonates with your true purpose,
Then you will be guided to act.
You are being asked to connect to Source energy
It is from there that you will receive your highest

There are many souls present
To guide you and accelerate your path
Excited to be of service
To assist in reaching your potential

And gravitate you toward the correct course
The world is yours for the asking
All you have to do is act
You are being guided from on high
Do not let doubt or worry hinder your progress
Great things are in store for you
State your desire and be open to assistance
Great things are in store for you
You must act when the moment strikes
You will be guided on each step
You must listen closely
You path will be revealed to you like the dawning of a new day
Greatness will be yours for the taking
You will give of yourself in a manner that will not deplete your
stores of energy
But replenish them with divine light and love
Take haste this day to retain the correct mindset
To remain open to messages that are coming in from on high.
This is your day, this is your glory
Receive it.
The light of the whole universe rests within your heart
Waiting to be granted permission to shine.
Open that door now.

You must find a way to liberate your mind
And free your intent
There is a storehouse of knowledge waiting to be accessed
within the regions of your cellular data
These will come to you in the form of dreams, memories and
visions
Do not be alarmed or resist in any way
Once you begin the ascension process your responsibility is to the
universe
You must pay heed the warnings you receive as well as the

messages of healing and light
Beware of the dark energy constructs that seek to destroy your
potential
These are the residuals of trauma
Do not feed them but release them into the healing love of the
universe
They will be forever altered and released

Release the guilt in your root chakra
Open to the divine love of the Great Mother
Imagine a spiral in your spine that begins in the earth
And extends to the top of your head
Open your heart to love
Release the inhibition, irritations

As you travel up through this ascension process
Your soul will reach through the layers and find healing
Reach for your higher self, always
Let the golden light surround you and keep you
Do not heed the darkness

Starseed you must open wide the floodgates of your heart
Stay strong, have courage
Goodness will prevail
Earth is no longer bound by chaos
But is a free and shining satellite as was intended
Now is your time to shine
Remember your soul's music
For it is the music of the gods
And ushers in a golden age

Remember your soul's beauty
For it is the beauty of all
A day of reckoning is upon us
Dark energy must flee
The sons and daughters of Earth will rejoice.

Your path will be bumpy
As you reach this acceding state
Every day will present a challenge
But if you take courage you will rise above
Call to yourself the lost fragments of Soul
These are your gift, your talent
Lying in dormant and waiting for the light of day
Yours is the path of greatness
Rise to meet it, child.

The time has come to for Earth and Starseed to reunite
These are the golden age of greatness
Expanded consciousness is upon the human race
May the blessing of the universe wrap you in love and light
May the music of the ages fill your soul
May the departed souls forever reunite with their twin flame
May the light carry you through this dark time as the world
paradigm shifts to love;
Blessings to all.

The time has come to for Earth and Starseed to reunite

A release is being offered to you:
The way out is through
And beyond your pain is immeasurable

Starseed
Your lesson today is to stay in a place of joy
Feed it into your heart, your neural network
Feel it pouring from your heart
Connect with your soul
Bring the golden light of your soul into your 3-D body
Revel at the simplicity in this new life path
There are no hardships here, only joy
There is no pain, only release
There is no fear, only the light of a new day
Each day is a gift
Treat it as such.

Starseed
Yours is the duty
Of calling your ancestral memories
To you and finding cohesion.
Your soul must activate these memories
Data stored at a cellular level
By heeding the calling of your heart

A bounty of blessings are all around you
Open your eyes and your heart to draw them into your reality
Align now with the will to act
Your lightbody is constricted by
Mental constructs of pain
In order to release them
You must be willing to shed
All that you think you know

And be reborn
There is a vast abyss
Between you and your whole conscious self
Make the leap
Find your wings
For you can fly.

◆ ◆ ◆

Starseed,
Your past and future are calling you as one
Are you ready?
Do not heed the pain
Do not feed the suffering
Release it as part of the transformation process
Let it help you recall your past
And nurture your future
There is much beauty beneath the pain of discovery
You must uncover the truth and set your mind free
You will be amazed at the beauty therein
You will find the wings to fly once again
The music that you hear is feeding you
The dance you long to be a part of is calling you
Become your future now
Anchor your soul within
Release the encumbrances of the past,
Find the blissful waters of your freedom.

Within you is a seed
That will be cultivated to greatness
How fast it grows is dependent on your willingness to reach
Beyond your current limitations
You are being called to act
In accordance with a higher plan.

This is your duty to the universe
Today you must act and you will manifest
All that is needed to continue on your path
The way will be shown;
Rise to meet it.

There are messages of light all around you,
Waiting to be encoded and brought to the surface
Of your memory bank.
Do not hesitate to embody these forms
They are planting the seeds
To greatness.
You must honor your path
You must find the key to unlocking
Your true potential;
Inside you are all the answers you need
The way will be shown.

You are being taken to a higher plane
To place perspective on your suffering.
You are being asked to open your heart chakra and release
suffering now;
There is no place for it in the beauty of the world.
From the smallest expression of energy to the largest life form,
All is constantly in a motion of love.
There are messages of light all around you in nature
The earth expresses her love in beautiful and unique forms
There is no fear, only acceptance
There is no phobia only the beautiful tickle of the spiders legs
That long to greet and feel your skin
Resonate now with us.
The fear you feel

Is holding you back from your potential.
For as truly as your heart reaches for your soul,
So does the heart of every living creature
And to find ecstasy in physical expression
Is to be god-like.
Open to the great possibilities that are within your grasp;
Move beyond a place of suffering.
Take heart and imagine your future
Along the bright highway of success;
Free from the encumbrances of fear and addiction.
You must release all the things that would hold you back.
Come into yourself now
Heed your own soul
Receive the light and love from all of us
Who are with you always.

◆ ◆ ◆

Take the time to heed these words
You must find the way
It lies in front of you
Waiting for discovery
You have hidden within yourself the gems of knowledge
That you can access at any point for the asking
Focus, open your heart and be willing to receive
The bounty of the earth surrounds you,
Eagerly awaiting your acceptance.
Stay steady and heed to the inner voice
It is the voice of your soul guiding you to greatness
Find a way to impart order and bring it into fruition
Everything you seek lies within your grasp
Take the time to heed the details
And slowly and steadily address each concern
And you will find the answers welling forth
From the springs of your heart
There is greatness to be had this day

You are being called to heed your higher self and complete your
mission
On satellite earth.

◆ ◆ ◆

It is possible to be godlike and humble
To retain the memory in our DNA
Clear your body of the blockages,
Release them one by one.
Open your heart and find the crystalline path.
Heed your body's need
Nourish your soul and nourish your mind
and the rest will fall into place
There is a well of joy within you that longs to bubble up
and taste the freedom of realization.
Release it now.

◆ ◆ ◆

Affirmation:
I am a being of light and love
I am activating now my soul's highest potential
Through the course of activation
My heart will feel heavy
My body will release the toxins of stored emotions
This is my soul's contract
To find a way to express my energy
in ways that reflect the highest order.

Fill your day with the joy of creation
Rejoice in your newfound path
Great riches lie waiting for the joy of discovery

Reach within yourself for the answers
Visualize the end results
You will find completion and success beyond your wildest dreams

Affirmation:
I will honor my soul's path
My mission is to share my gift with others
In ways that are favorable to my spirit and health.
To bring to fruition these ideas I must act
I align myself with the will to act
I align myself with the joy of success
I release my inhibitions into the ether and align myself with the
joy of the universe
That awaits my comprehension.
The beauty that wells within me is the beauty of the world
Longing to be shared and tasted and lingered in
I awaken now my soul purpose with passion and commitment
Breaking through all the constructs of perceived boundaries
Their release conditions me for greatness
I will complete my mission and honor my path
I will seek to love and spread love
And share the beauty of my soul with the world.

Child
Rest awhile
Find your divinity and grace
You were made for big, important journeys,
You will find the path through rest.
Ease your fears, let them run through you like water.
Drink water, flush your body
Renew your spirit
Receive vitality from the universe,

Our gift to you this day.
Rest your mind
Unburden your soul
Let the cares of the world wash away
Just for today

You are a divine being of light
Clothed in mortality
Nurture your divinity as you would a small babe
Let it shine from within and enhance everything you do
In turbulent times it will protect you from the chaos.
Let it cloak you in goodness,
So all that you touch becomes a golden manifestation of your inner light.
Let life bloom across you
Take a moment to taste the sweetness
There is no need to rush
You have everything you need to succeed
Shape your belief to the point of acceptance
And results will follow
There will always be those who do not understand,
Do not let that dim your brightness.

There is a point starseed
Where your dreams will become a reality because of, or in spite of your best efforts
For so long you have focused on your aim
That your subconscious mind is manifesting without your consent
Worry not and act as though it is already yours
For in this state of content will you find your way
The path lies before you; a gleaming opportunity

That will carry you to your destination with great speed
Yours is the path of success.
Let yourself Become
Taste the sweetness life has to offer
Ride above the crashing waves and feel the golden sun
Warming your back
There is no need to worry,
All will come to you in due time
Heed nothing but the inner urges that bring you closer to your dreams
These are calling you to your home
All that you long for is but a few breaths away
Arise and cloak yourself in the mantle of success
Your dreams are calling you;
Heed them.

Your subconscious is an axis,
On which your life is pivoting.
Continue to feed it well
And the ensuing beauty and creation will forever ripple outward
In glorious manifestations of beauty and light.
There is so much love and goodness in you
Radiating from your core
It is time to share this goodness with others
The world needs more light
A way shower and bringer of happy tidings
Err on the side of love and your abundance will follow
Still your mind and the beauty therein
Will blossom out onto your life
Peace and happiness are yours for the asking
Reach for these and goodness will follow
Still the chaos and in the rubble you will find the answers you seek
Let yourself Become

Your destiny is carving its way through the best possible variables
Be prepared to accept fruition with grace
The way will be shown to you in the stillness
Let your reach extend far and god-like
For greatness is yours for the asking.
Do not hesitate to ask and open your heart to receive.

◆ ◆ ◆

Your senses will block an average delight
A special moment of space found in between
The larger moments of laughter and love
Heed these quiet chunks of time
The space between is what fills you with joy and fuels your progress
Heed the stillness,
Therein lie the answers you seek.
In the quiet of the mind is a fountain of knowledge
Primed and ready for use
Eagerly awaiting your acceptance and realization
Realize now your divinity
Your innate connection to God
The core of goodness that resides within you
Here is your strength, here are your roots
Deeply embedded in the Mother
Trust that you can make it happen
And so it will be.
Trust you are free,
And so you shall be.

How can we explain your goodness
In showering glimmering bits of golden light
Radiating from your energy field
Transposing so much beauty into the atmosphere

There is a line
Between the known and unseen
Begin to cross it now.
Feel with your heart
All that you know but refuse to acknowledge.
Before you lies a threshold,
You must cross it.
Feel the warmth radiating from your core of intimate knowing
Inside you lies the key
To unlock the door of your subconscious and enter your truth
Forget the cares and worries for a moment
And drift with us,
Ethereal, plasma, energy and light
Buffeted by cosmic winds
Standing ever close to your soul.
Release the negative energy now into the the cosmic force
Let it drain away from you now
You are protected by divine light.

Dear one
You come with many questions
But the answers you seek are already in you
Never doubt the source
Release the negative thoughtforms
That are hindering your progress
To stay with your peace
You must cast off the shackles that are impeding you
These are worry, fear, stress, control.
You must relinquish these all to the universal force
And let your energy realign with your life purpose
Your destiny is calling you
Your dreams await your realization
Heed them
Reach for your home, find the sweet spot

And nestle there in safety and love
Steady your mind with your breath
In the stillness your intuition will guide

❖ ❖ ❖

You are faced with a set of obstacles of your own choosing
As you traverse the layers of reality
You will find many spots of tension
Release them and move on
The way spreads out before you
A glistening spiral of energy and light
you will feel the pulsing urge from within,
You must heed it.
For within you lies
A fountain of beauty and joy
resting beneath your biggest inhibition.

❖ ❖ ❖

Yours is a path of beauty and light
Stay in the moment and heed the small nudges from within
Succumb not to temptations all around you
Reach for strength and excellence
And it will reflect in all your dealings
Beneath the sluggish roots
There is a flow of energy and grace
Treat your body well

❖ ❖ ❖

Worry not for the many fears that pop into your mind.
These are the residual traces of negative thoughtforms you are
releasing.
Let them disperse on the horizon,

17

Fragments of dark clouds scattering in the wind.
Worry not and embrace the day
Heed the tugs of creative force
These are the inspirations that will bring you joy
And guarantee your success

◆ ◆ ◆

Child you must act
Now is the time for fruition
Your dreams are calling you
Fill your heart with goodness and hold it there
Do not let others dissuade you
Stay true to your goals
Your dreams are calling you, do not hesitate
Now is the time to leap
Release your inhibitions
These shadows that flit across your mind
Are of your own making
There is nothing stopping your success
Release your fears
And fly
Dance with us
Elemental energies
Inexorably bound to fleet and tumble
With the matter of your thoughts
Let your thoughts be rich and pure
Greatness is yours for the asking
You must uncover your true nature
And let your heart shine as it was meant to

Your soul is calling you to act
The earth is calling you to dance
In divine co-creation

Joy, peace and contentment are yours for the asking
Open your heart to receive the bounty of the universe
This is the day you will receive great blessings
Stay open and let your heart receive
A bounty of good is coming your way
There is much this day has to offer if you will slow down to look
Remember your progress
And honor the completion you have found
There is much joy to be had in the simple things
Give freely of yourself and you will open the way for receiving
Open your heart to the love that longs to pour from you
There is nothing to fear
Light and truth and honor surround you
Your soul is seeped in integrity
You must honor your path
Find a quiet place and prepare yourself
For this marvelous day.

Your future is calling you
Reach not outward but inward
Inside you is the core of knowing
Within is the seat of knowledge and goodness
That resides in the base of your spine
Seek the bodhi spot and you will find
Joy beyond measure
And peace everlasting
This is your destiny of greatness
And your place of understanding
You must access it now

Relax your spine and feel your cares and worries
Melt into the ground

There is a spot of sweetness
You must reside there and activate
Your inner knowing
Approach all things from this place of calm
Begin now to build this habit
And it will ingrain itself into your soul
And all your dealings will be peaceful.

❖ ❖ ❖

Do not doubt your divine connection
Even if you can not actively feel it
It is always present
Connect to the vital source of energy through your spine
That is surging from the earth and longing to rush through you
And fill you with joy and vitality
Connect now to this source
You must lift the veil you have shrouded yourself in
And come into your knowing
Release the petty differences
And recognize oneness and divine purpose
Pulsing through your life and seeking fulfillment
Release your anger or lack of understanding
You cannot undo the past
You cannot hide from the truth
You must embrace your destiny
Your home is calling you
Ride above the storm child
The crashing waves were meant to bolster you up
There is a sweet spot here in the golden sun
You must find it now

Child do not force the feelings
Let them ebb and flow naturally

This journey through healing is for you to savor
And delight in.
Release your guilt and shame
It impedes your progress
We are here to remind you of your glorious goodness,
The elemental core of zeal that resides within you.
Release your pain
And uncover the joy therein
It longs to spring everlasting
Bolstering you up into the golden light
Of your soul's wisdom
These things you must do:
Breath
Let yourself feel joy
Your soul longs to dance with us,
Golden elemental energy
Drifting on cosmic winds.
It is your life your path
Of oneness and connection to all
Be here now.

◆ ◆ ◆

This place you call home
Rests in your heart
Open it to receive
And greatness will be yours

◆ ◆ ◆

Your soul asks you
To remove the inhibitions from your aura
And find freedom in expression
There are beliefs holding you
in places of fear and denial of your goodness
Reconsider the position of these barriers

Perhaps they are meant to be lessons and released
Perhaps they are already behind you
You must allow yourself the freedom you seek
It is right there in front of you
A simple cowl to cast about you
Disguise yourself in it
And it will become your permanent reality
Place before you now
Your visions of success and positivity
Let them seep into your consciousness
You are reprogramming your mind to compute in a different way
Big changes are in the making
Seeking the truest expression of your soul
Act from love and goodness will always follow
Walk in grace and freedom you will find

Cast aside your worries, doubts and inhibitions,
Release them now into the plasma
That surrounds you always
Ethereal energy comingling with yours
Direct it to work in your favor
Through your breath.
You will find repetition forms a habitual way
Of being present and mindful
Stay in the goodness and light
There is much for you to accomplish yet
Your life will collect a different hue
And you will find daily joy is attainable
The future is rising up to meet you
Are you ready to embrace your calling?

Walk in grace and focus on your breath

Begin to draw your success toward you
It is ripe and awaiting your enjoyment
Begin now to breath in awareness
Heed the little pops of inspiration that come to you
These are the making of your success
Endeavor to stay mindful and in the moment
Aware of your feelings and Self
As two separate entities
Realize now your power
Wrap it around you
It will shield you from trials and tribulations
Your success hinges on your ability to remain mindful
Let the surface distractions wash away
Stay rooted in yourself
You have all you need to succeed

These blocks you hold around you
Must be released
Release your attachment to the ideals
That secure them in place
They are like cords that will bind you
Draw away from them with your breath
Cleanse your aura now
Your greatness is calling you
Will you heed it?

Your soul sees your worth
Even when you fail to do so
Begin now to embrace the light
Begin now to reach for your goodness
There is a sweet spot inside of you
You must nestle there and protect yourself

From life's storms
Release the fear you hold deep within
you have so much to give
You are a golden fountain of love and goodness
Let it flow from you now and always.
Forgive yourself your transgression
And allow yourself to breathe in goodness
This is the life you chose
Full of trials
To hone you into the beautiful and straight arrow you are today
Release yourself now and fly to your dreams
Your aim in true and steady
Your heart is evermore guided by love
Your abilities are boundless
Your happiness awaits
Accept it now as your just reward
Honor the beauty and riches in your life
Imagine your relationships full of light and love
And so they shall be.
Move with grace let your steps be light on the earth
There is much joy within your grasp;
Access it now.

◆ ◆ ◆

Child inside you is a seed
Awaiting fruition
Now is the time to accept the changes in your life
They are happening rapidly beneath the surface
Ready to burst through
You must tend to your soul and water your dreams
Little by little they will reach realization
There is a sweetness in your soul
That is much loved by those around you
And us in the spirit realm,
We are attracted to your golden glowing light

Like moths to an open flame.
We dance around you and play in your soul's light
Dance now with us
Lighten your load
your blockages are a deceit
They are not true to your nature
Uncover your potential
A sharp sword that will cut through the illusion
You are much more than you realize
Break the shackles of fear that bind you
These are residuals of a much darker past
They are no longer contained in your current reality
Do not let the darkness deceive you
Reach for the light
It is yours for the asking
You are powerful and godlike in ability
You must uncover your potential now.

Child changes are happening rapidly
You must slow down with your breath
Let your breathing guide you through tumultuous situations
Do not entertain thoughts of destruction and violence
Do not let your heart be troubled
Visualize instead how you wish it to be
Your thoughts are powerful tools
More real than you comprehend.
Let not your heart be worried
For this day and every day you will shine
Like the bright star you were meant to be
Do not let the perceptions of others
Clog your energy flow
Remain here with us in the ethereal
Dancing forever in the light of the golden sun
You are boundless, godlike

Reach now for goodness,
Dance with us.

Your time is golden
And slowed down
By an inner mechanism you must access
With your breath
The path to success is glowing before you
You must arise and meet the challenge
Life is presenting you
A perfect puzzle of your own making
Rise now and find your success
Within you are all the answers you will ever need
Trust your instinct and heed your inner knowing
You must rise up and create the life you want
In joy and simplicity
Rejoice in the challenge
For you have found your authentic path.

Stay in the love
And see clearly your own blocks
Begin now to release them into the ether
Your time is golden and blessed
Release your love and it will come back to you tenfold
Step into your power child
The time to rise is now
You are deserving of grace
You have proven your path
Through hard work and patience and love
Arise now to conquer
Accept now that you are deserving of greatness
And it will be yours

Let your beauty shine onto the world
So that others may follow in your footsteps
Begin now.

Now is your time to rise
You must access your core of greatness
Release your doubts and inhibitions
These are frequencies holding you back
From realizing your goals
Raise your vibrational field
And remain there
It will buffer you from the annoyances
Or grievances that clog your spiritual path
Use your voice
To heal your body
You must break through the complacency
That is clogging your energy field
This invisible cloak of sorrow or sadness must be released into the
ether
You are no longer a product of your past
You have reinvented yourself
Now is your time to shine.

Rise up child and meet your destiny
Shirk no more the urges that are calling you
You must still the chatter
To gain clarity
Begin now to say:
I am a transcendental being full of love and light
I possess all of the strengths necessary to complete my tasks
I am loving and divine
I feel my strength permeate from my core

I am protected and loved

Find your inherent joy
Release your anger and frustration
For beneath lies a wealth of creative influx
You must adapt a new view
You must exercise your calm
Realize your freedom now
There is no obligation to be angry
You must release with compassion and joy
At finding your authentic path.
Your voice will be heard,
If you let it be so.
Do not focus your anger through a pinhole,
When you can give it to the sky.

there are many things to rejoice in
So let not your heart be heavy
For the season of sadness has passed
Before you lies your destiny
Take heart and stay firm in your joy
Do not let the trials and tribulations of others
Dim your your light
Seek out the things that bring you satisfaction
Of completion and rebirth
Replant the old ideas fueled by anger
And let them be grown into love.
Within lies the key to your success
You must heed your inner urges
If you listen you will be nudged in the right direction
Take the first step

Your soul wishes to reunite with your true earth mission
Clean your body, free your mind
The world is waiting on your success
You have a part to play that is vital for the success of all
A necessary piece of the larger puzzle
Release your ego
Give yourself permission to fly
your quest for answers
Will block the truth in front of you
You must step into your truth
the answers you seek
Are all within
If you will slow down to listen
The block you perceive is of your own making
Placed of your free will
Just easily you can remove it.
Ask it to leave,
It does not serve you
Nor is it your duty to bear this stone
Toss it into the ocean depths.

Worry not for the uncompleted tasks
Reach within for strength and fortitude
Gather your resources about you
For these will guide you home
There is a small portion of your heart
That is clouded by sadness
You must release it into the ethereal
Let yourself be guided
Do not resist the messages coming to you

We are here to assist you in finding your authentic path
Reach for your soul
Shining and golden in the universal aftermath
Of collison and rebirth
Contractions and expansions that birthed your presence
Breath with us
there is nothing to fear
You are an open conduit of goodness and light

Hold now within you this peace
Let it guide your day and fill your soul
There is no lack only love
Seek fulfillment through your thoughts and let your actions express them.
Do not walk the fool's path along the precarious edge
Stay in the light
You are protected and loved
There are many souls vying for your success
You must heed them and release your efforts to block their assistance
Raise your vibration
Reach for the sunlight
Do not aid the darkness any longer
You are a child of God,
You must step into your heritage.
Resistance changes to acceptance `
Through your breath and your belief;
Exercise these now.

The dawn of a new age has begun
It is time for lightworkers of the world to unite in forces
There is much work to be done

The darkness spills from the universe
and reaches across our souls
In heaviness
This is the weight of distance
The heaviness is gravity
The sadness is how you choose to see this weight as a burden
Reach for the sunlight always present
Even in the vastness of space the ethereal golden light particles
Dance on the cosmic winds
feel them now
Let your burdens be lightened
for the universe rejoices
In this new age

◆ ◆ ◆

Step into your power
Worry not for you are a child of gods
The fleeting thoughts in your mind
Are remnants of an old belief system
Release them with your breath
Within your core
There is a place of calm
Step into this now.

◆ ◆ ◆

Dear one
You are being asked to put aside petty differences
Do not let the words of strangers elicit your response
We are all the children of god
They are fulfilling their destiny
It is not for you to decide their morality
Release your anger and embrace the compassion
And love welling up in your heart
For within you are a treasure trove of information

If you must share a message, let it be love.

◆ ◆ ◆

Stay in the beauty
This day you will accomplish great things
If you permit yourself to be joyful
Here are your tasks:
Begin in love
Release your fear
Reach into your future
Walk in mindfulness
Know that you are God
And from you springeth life
Which is the life force of everything
Embrace your inherent godlike nature
Become who you truly are

◆ ◆ ◆

Child, stay in the light.
Connect to the Earth
She will nourish you
Find a space to create
For greatness can be yours this day
Open your heart to love
Rise above the waves
And stay in your joy
There is much to celebrate in passing
There is much life that death brings
Release your tears to the Earth,
She will hold you close.
The Earth grid is active
And calling you to connect and join in the sacred dance
Discover your bliss and the numbness will peel away.
Within your heart

Is an ever flowing fountain of goodness and joy
Linger there
What brings you joy
What will rekindle the light in your heart and fire in your soul
Creation is calling you
Worry not for completion
The time is not yet come
You must walk through your current cycle
With grace

Child call forth the fire
Of anger and passions unrealized
Let it burn away complacency now
Etch your purpose with the flame
Hone your instinct
sharpen your sword of understanding
Cut away the fog
Wooly remains of lingering karmic vestiges
Fading away into the ether
Loosened of their hold

Child you must see your goodness
Wrap it around you in a shield of golden light
Let the last vestiges of healing emerge
Release those old inhibitions
You are right to grieve
Go forward to new land
The dawn of a new age awaits
Embrace it now.
There is a karma in forgiveness
That extends beyond this lifetime
Releasing old debts or contracts

Or generational ties
Ushering in the way for love and healing
Releases your karmic debt.

Rise up child and greet the new day
This and many more will bring you great blessings
If you only allow yourself to receive
The worries that clog your aura
Are but residuals of a past that no longer
Fits your reality
The situations you have surrounded yourself in
Are soul contracts
Awaiting your acknowledgement and release
When you have fulfilled your obligation, then the contract is closed
And you can move on to embrace your destiny
It is wild and calling you
To join in a joyous dance
Of creation and visualization
Of light and manifestation
If a contract brings you suffering,
You must absorb the lesson and release.
Address it full on with courage and wisdom
Send the situation light and love
And release with love

Let your worries fall away
Embrace this dance with constant need for growth and visualization
This is what you longed for
Ever needing one more part of you to extend beyond your normal reach

If you connect to the Earth you will find your center of calm
And be revitalized and rejuvenated
Let your soul be content knowing you have all that you need
To create a perfect life

Child lay aside that which ails you
Always reach for the golden light of the universe
Toward healing and grace
Find the center of your balance and rest there
Encircled by the energy of Gaia
Find your point of least resistance and nudge it in the proper
direction
There is much healing you have unearthed in your continual
process of rebirth and regeneration.
You must recognize your current healing process for what it is
Do not assign labels to it
Do not create attachments
Just let it go with grace
These are the dredges of soul brought to light
Release with love

Rise with a glad heart to meet your soul
The angels are singing in your praise
Release the sadness
There are many here to aid you on your journey
Let joy and peace and love fill your heart
And optimize your energy transmission
Seek the answers in small moments
Reach for the golden light always
Control your emotions through your breath
Drink water for optimal energy transmission
You must maintain

A proper energy balance in alignment with your goals
High protein and hydration will help you achieve your optimal
state.
Rise to meet your challenges with a glad heart

Joy becomes you
Imprinted on the corners of your life
Filling up your days with sunshine
Joy is the language of nature
The seedling rising through the dirt to meet the sun
Joy in the conquest of predator and prey
For you also there is joy abundant
Let your spirit now rejoice
In the healing of the planet
The healing of your body
There is much thanks to give and joy to be had

Child you must release the last bit of energy clogging your aura
There is peace and joy eternal on the other side
Troubles will be yours no longer
You must release with joy and stay steady on your path of healing
The roadblocks you encounter are of your own creation
Learn to step around them with grace
You are protected, safe and cherished
Your energy is vital to this planet
Your ideas and creations will help the Earth heal
As your body settles into this new phase of healing
Blocked emotions will emerge
Cling not to them
But release them with joy unto the universe
The angels are dancing with your joy
All of creation sings along with you

Stretching ever toward eternal bliss
Let not your heart be troubled

Take joy in the little things
Think of the love all around you;
Revel in your bliss.
Your loneliness is a result
Of looking ahead instead of within
Release the need to know
And let your days fall with grace
Laughter will buffer you against the trials

Rest in the earth and let your roots branch out
Your spirit will guide you in all things now
Reach out for assistance as needed
Stay in a place of rest and growth
Nothing is needed but for you to heal
And release the tangle that has you bound
Let your roots stretch and be free
Encumbered no more by guilt or shame
Or other trappings placed upon you
Forgive, release and shine
Rise to meet this golden day
Let the sun warm your upturned face
and may your heart blossom goodness
There is much joy within you bottled up and ready to explode
Across your life in a myriad of ways
Great things are coming
You must be grounded to receive

Child the time has come for you to heal
Lay aside the trappings of must and should
And replenish your vitality through water and rest
Slow down
In your haste your thoughts tumble like a waterfall
Let them pool and find yourself dipping into their still waters
There are solutions there for every problem you perceive
Healing is within your grasp
All the answers that you seek
Are within you

Let your spirit drift above the turbulence
On the wings of an Eagle
Fly high and look down with keen eye
See the direction in which you want your life to go
Examine what it is you really want
And set a plan of action
Thus releasing stressors generated by the unknown
Clearly adhere to your path
Therein will you find joy
And follow your hearts desires
Let not the turbulence
Dissuade you from your path
Stay focused and follow the guidance offered to you
Your destination is greatness
There is no limit to the things you will achieve
Open your heart to receive

Let joy in
You are poised on the edge of greatness

You must begin to stay in a place of joy
Like a muscle that must be exercised
You must stay steady and constant and train your thoughts
To receive joy and happiness
Quit shrinking into and begin filling out your space
Your perspective is beginning to shift in powerful directions
Joy is the acceptance of all things exactly as they come
With no need to alter or change them
A clear mind and untroubled heart
Can reach boundless heights
Begin now to sit with your joy
And accept it for the vast and nameless feelings
There is no fear of falling
But of buoyancy
You will be lifted into the heavens in ecstasy
Remain in this place daily
And see the fruits of your labor blossom and ready for harvest

The world is a vast space
Filled with incarnating souls
Seeking understanding of their existence
Each on evolutionary paths that lead
To personal fulfillment
It is not your place to decide the right or wrong of their journey
But to garner your own energy and tend your own soul
For vast are the riches of the joyful heart
And untroubled mind
To sit in reverence daily is a gift that your soul has long sought
To breath in the wonder of your existence
And revel in the bee touching the flower
Is a privilege sought by many
Let your fears drift away
And release the doubts that have you backtracking
Release the burdens that express through other souls

and obligations that do not bring you fulfillment
You sit abreast a pinnacle of shining truth
And brighten a dark world
Do not be discouraged if others do not see your light
It is not their path to do so
Sit among those who take joy in your truth
And you will be rewarded with friendships
Whose value is greater than gold
Do not attempt to go back and mend the past
Let it flow away in the river
That always seeks to join the vastness of the sea

◆ ◆ ◆

Do not lose your softness
In a hard world you must approach yourself with love
Step beyond a linear view of yourself
And open to the possibility that you are all of the things you were
simultaneously existing and seeking fulfillment.
You must love each piece of the past to find cohesion
These divergent parts will come together to create a beautiful
whole
Your anger and fear are directed at your inner child
Remove these weapons you have pointed at your frailest moments
And revel in your strength to withstand such storms and remain
intact
Is the anger your own
Or a conditioning placed upon you by your father
Who could not stoop to love his own child self
Forgive him and embrace yourself

◆ ◆ ◆

In the light of morning
The darkness of the world appears to release it's hold
Do not fret the darkness

For it is the underside of light
In a new day give thanks for your beingness

You are a child of Gods
Made perfect in their image
How you choose to express that image onto the world
In joy or suffering
Both are aspects of divinity
It is in overcoming our suffering that true character is revealed
Set aside your vices
Stay on the path of wonder
And great riches will be yours for the asking
Rise into the yellow morning light
And claim it as your own
Acknowledge your right to be fulfilled
It is your birthright to be free
And return to a place of knowing and peace

There is a time
To mourn things and to celebrate their passing
Find within you now a place to safely store your sorrow
When the time comes you can return it to the earth
In light and love
Within the vast storehouse of your mind
There is a hidden gem of knowledge
Begin now to understand your mission here on earth
And recall the soul contract that binds you to your mortality
For within you are the answers you seek
The search for answers will destroy the hidden knowledge
Access your divinity
And you will find your answer

◆ ◆ ◆

Within your mind
There is a seed that must be planted
You must foster compassion
Let is bloom across your life
In full array of senses
Align yourself with the compassion of the universe
That does not push the flower to grow
But gently tickles the unfurling petals
With wind and rain and sun
Take your lesson from the earth
Follow the ways of nature
And in time it will become your nature as well
Always seek to understand the lesson
Within nature there is freedom
The daisy does not worry to unfurl beside a rose
Each equal in their right to reach for sun
And root through the earth

People of earth
We are one
Your consciousness is but the stored consciousness of all
Much like the human body exists as a series of separate enzymatic
reactions
So is the human consciousness
Each a necessary part of the whole
Visualize the human race as a body
And your individuality is but a cell within that magnificent whole
Your struggle is the struggle of all
Your sorrow is shared across the vast consciousness of all
Your joy is expressed through the flower bursting forth from a bud
We are one

Within life there is a center of joy
It can be activated through an energetic connection to your planet
Your dna contains the source codes
To connect with satellite earth
This joy is vital to the growth and expansion of the universe
For within your chaos exists a structure
You are responsible for bringing into reality the expansion of
another universe
The souls teeming your planet are fulfilling their karmic mission
for even chaos and destruction
feeds life that must evermore expand and bloom
The temporal reality that you call existence is but a fragment of
universal truth
But a minute faction in an ever spinning wheel of
recovery and discovery
Give and take
Growth and disease
Light and darkness
People of the earth will unite
And rise together singing as one voice
To usher in the dawning of a new age
People of Earth heed this
The day of your life reckoning is drawing near
There will be no more room for denial of your Source connection
Love is calling you
Will you surrender?

A dawning of a new age is upon us
People of earth will taste the glorious nectar of awakening
Rob not your spirit of knowledge
Seek evermore the fruits of the garden

For this is your day to bring to light that which has been hidden
for centuries
People of earth rejoice
We are one
Earth must rise up as one
Singing one song
Starseeds unite
And show the way
Your mission is to heal the earth
And assist her birthing process
Human consciousness must shift:
The planet is trying to save her children.

Child release your resistance
You must use your breath as a tool to open your mind
Within you is a vast garden
Full of hidden treasure troves of knowledge
Meld now in this cellular dance
A cosmic shifting of consciousness
That expands all space and time.
To sit in reverence is a gift;
Open your spine to let it become a conduit of goodness and
healing.
The trivialities that draw you back into a point of tension
Are but dramas playing out across a stage.
The key is to release this energy in the form of creation
Within that pinnacle point where soul meets expressions of love
Is the secret to your true power
There is healing to be found for you this day
And continued release of your resistance
The earth heals through you child
Within each of you is the key to all life
In the form of energy potential
You must unite as one and activate the planet

Through your genetic code
There is a shift coming
For good or bad is determined within each of you
Your human body is capable of far more than you could imagine
It is a tool to activate Mother Earth
She sustains you and gives you life
It is through the bowels of the earth that you transmit your energy
Hear me now
A day draweth closer ever still toward extinction of your species
To survive you must unite;
It is within unity you will find a way.
The purpose of humanity is to grow and express love

Oh child, to hold this present moment is such a gift.
Affirmation:
I breathe in the ecstasy of recognition
I breathe out toxins of past lives
Remnants of lost realities
Always this breath
Always this Soul, this presence
This rapture
How my Soul does rejoice at it's expression
How my joy does lift me.

To activate your soul mission,
You must align yourself with the spirit of doing.
Your body is healing and releasing toxins
As you release your emotions
So does your chemistry change and fluctuate
You must be ready to rise and meet these changes
This gift of light you have chosen to receive
Is your destiny unfolding

Be patient and do not search for answers
But let them come to you in the stillness
Within your brain there is a vast treasure trove of information,
Awaiting assimilation.

The now presents your greatest potential
Within your brain your neurons exist in a state
That is activated by the full potentiality of the moment
The chemistry of your body is lacking only awareness to achieve
it's optimal states
Within each cell
Is imprinted a dna memory of full resolution
To access your truest healing potential you must remain in the
present.

Child the song in your heart is the language of nature
As does nature express in bird song
Or rustling of wind through trees
So does your heart sing, so do your cells tingle;
So is your spirit made buoyant.

The waves are but constructs of true energy in its purest form
Within you is a similar tide of advance and retreat
Magnetic fluctuations that exist within each cell of your body
Each an entire world of its own,
Each existing in harmonious balance.

That you wish to hear from without is within you
A message of love written across your soul;
You are love and life.

The message you seek is written in your breath
Encoded in your eyes
Uploaded through the sunlight glancing off the leaves
You are love and life
Within you is everything you need
To move past your obstacles with ease
Begin now to see your true power
Begin to unveil those gifts that were given you
Call your dreams into reality
Release the mental fluctuations
Let the golden light of the sun enshroud you always.

Child the wellness within you
Will ripple outward onto your life.
Accept now the loving glow of your universal soul,
Who wishes to extend to you the
Light and joy of healing and health.

Within you wells a goodness
Let it cover your life in a flowing rush of light
Be Here Now
Let it emanate form the core of your being
And wrap all that you do in glowing goodness
The patience you seek is waiting to be realized
Your soul's mission is calling you

Within you child is a light

You must continue to shine it on the dark places
The healing in your spine
Will open up your deeply rooted fears
And release them into the ether
Your Soul family is calling you
All around you is humanity
Needing the divine light
Of universal love
Connect with the earth
And become an open conduit
Of healing energy.
Around you is an embroiled mass
Of simmering, repressed emotions
Bubbling to the surface
As the human race strives for healing and grace
It is through the broken places in you
That your healing light will shine
As you realize your pain,
So do you realize the pain of all
As you heal yourself
So do you heal all.
Let your beauty unfold
Like the blossom opening to the sun
Be not afraid to shine and show your true worth
Which is all the weight of the world in gold.

Within the core of humanity lies a seed of life
This seed is ever fed by divine energy
And nurtured properly will grow into a massive tree of collective
consciousness
The key to peace among your species is to gather together your
minds as one mind
The energy encapsulating each fiber of your being is but a part of
the energy of the whole

The urges within you to heal and create
Are your driving forces you must honor them
Let not your light dim
But rekindle the fire of your creative seat
And feel the connection to Source energy
It is now time to move beyond the energetic weight of your past
And release it into the plasma.
Feel now the buoyancy of your soul dancing forever in the golden
light

Away from the darkness
Must you guide your precious energy
Your time on earth is short
Spend it enjoying your days
Or you will die with regrets.

You are seen and loved
The impact of your loving vibration ripples into the ether
Do not fret for things you cannot control
Feel the glow of the eternal sunlight
Within your core is a tightness
You must facilitate its release
Breath into it and pull from it the toxins
That hold you in stasis
Blow them into the ether
And let the buoyancy of joy eternal fill you.

Child you must listen to your body
That longs to stand on the earth

Hands in the water
Hair wet with rain
Lips curved by the wind
This wild inside you
Is a joy so pure
And savage
That it will rip what you know to shreds
And leave you heaving
Wide open
No lies or secrets
All is bared
All is alive
Pulsing with joy

You are a creature of light and love
Within you reside two polar extremes
You choose between the two at any given point
The secret of your training is to learn to walk steady
Between the two
Do not throw the chemicals in your brain off
Those are meant to assist you in your learning process
Every atom and particle in your body
Is geared toward bringing you into synchronicity with your life
mission
You must remain open to the possibility that you are exactly
where you need to be
Following the divine plan laid out before you
Your search for answers will awaken within you a restless energy
That will consume you
You must be patient and accept what is in front of you this day,
this moment
Do not abandon your dreams because you cannot see their
fruition
But instead find a way to restructure your intention

And rearrange the outcome.
Until you learn to be in your present,
You deny yourself the joy that is your driving force.

Let not grief cloud your precious energy field
Within you are the workings of greatness
Rest easy child and know that your greatness is but slumbering
You must find the key to awaken it within you
And bring it roaring to the surface
The key to your suffering is to transmute it into love
The key to your sorrow is to find the the buried joy
The key to your longings is to create a life that fulfills them
Your loneliness will be no more if you only open your chakras wide
And let the loving light of the universe guide you to a place of gratitude
And fellowship
Garner now your strength and release the ego's manifestation of suffering

Child within you is a spiral of light
Weaving up from the base of your spine
It's many tendrils weaving around every aspect of your life
You must unentangle yourself from the toxicity
that you have allowed yourself to become embroiled with
Simply envision the strands pulling back untie the knots
And free yourself from the darkness
There will always be darkness
But so much more is the light
Full of goodness and purity
And all of the things which bring you joy
Breathe into the moment

Hold yourself tender
And know that this is all a necessary expansion of consciousness
You are traveling upward into the many layers and dimensions of
your 3-D reality
There will be a time when you inner work will begin to shine
A light so bright you will no longer
Be able to conceal it
You must ride with the tides of energy that are pulling you ever
closer to your true purpose
The fear you feel is the fear of the planet
Become a conduit now and release it into the ether
There is much to love and much to do to fill your days with joy

Good is coming
You must be patient
Your burdens are about to lift
Long you have waited for your chance to shine in the sun
Your life will become pleasantly full and ripe
And pregnant with promise
Within you are all the answers you need to live a successful life
There is much pain in your body to release
It is residuals of suffering
You must welcome the pain
As you would an olde and tiresome friend
Sit with it, listen to it's woes and release it on its way
Within the core of your being
Your life energy is longing to release
It will consume you in a burning fervor
Your life is coming in full circle
Heed the signs and dreams
These are your directions along the way
There is much left for you to do
You have not fully begun to live your potential
Your fears are still holding you back

Name them and release them into the ether

There is a space between healing and the moment
A place so vital to sit and breathe it in
To honor the process you must breathe.
Affirmation:
Before me many have marched thousands and millions of ancestors
Egg and sperm meeting as one
Cells joining
An endless succession of creation to bring me here
In this moment
Alive and breathing in my joy
I am rapture
I am the eternal bliss of water molecule at last meeting with the shore
I am a breath, a life, a consciousness
A beating heart
This body is my anchor
Above it all my soul does dance in the joy of discovery.

Long will the light of soul shine
You must release your fears of death and aging
And embrace the life that spreads out before you
Glistening in the morning sun
Long have you sought and worked for the things you have
Breathe into the present and allow yourself to feel joy

You have been sleeping child
Nestled in a cocoon of healing

Drifting between consciousness and primordial urges
Life and death
Sickness and health
Mental fluctuations that have prevented you from realization
That you are on the precipice
Poised for flight
Within are all the necessary ingredients needed for your success
You must put your knowledge to action
It is through action that you will find escape from your lethargy
The mire of healing and suffering has long weighed you down
You must rise and embrace your courageous spirit
That longs to laugh and dance carefree in the light of day
Let this go and you will be amazed and awed at the person you
become
So light and full of love
No longer weighed down by regrets and suffering
Your healing is complete for now child
Let yourself enjoy and revel in your hard work
The time has come to dance and rejoice in the life spreading before
you
So rich and sweet and full of love
You must honor your inherent joy
Take action, begin to take the first step in faith
The rest will follow naturally

◆ ◆ ◆

The way has opened up before you
A long road slow and winding
You will walk it alone at times
But your diligence will be rewarded
This is your time
To breathe in those things which bring you joy
And release the last residuals of pain
Your energy has shifted into a higher frequency
You are now operating from a place of boundless joy

This joy becomes you
And paints your energy field with a myriad of colors
That is a joy to witness
Within you the seed has been planted
As it takes root and grows you will be amazed
At the beauty that is your life

Begin to open yourself to answers
And all the particulars will fall into place
Like the gentle summer breeze that settles fallen debris
Do not mourn their fall, for they were meant to end this way
You must reconcile your fears with the light of the sun
You must find a way to accept the truth that will be revealed
To stay in a place of love
Your time to shine is now

Your gift will at times feel like a burden
As it weeds out the insincere and scatters false motives
Your presence is needed
In a world lost in chaos
Anger and fear have become motivating forces
There is still time to love
You must reach for it and hold aloft its golden light
You will never err in the path of love

Your gift will at times feel like a burden
As it weeds out the insincere and scatters false motives

To begin you must rid your body of impurities
Your food and drink are sacred treat them as such
And revel in their nourishment
Hydrate your body

These words are not laid out as judgements
But as guides to supplement your body, mind and soul
Your human nature must take into account all the biological,
mental and emotional fluctuations
That make you the unique individual that you are
Heed not the tugging of guilt but instead release it into the
atmosphere
Your path is beautiful and chaotic
You must step away from the chaos and noise and ride above your
life
There you will receive a clearer picture
Become a hawk and warm your feathers in the sun
There is much for you to accomplish and fill your days with joy
A sense of purpose and determination is waking up inside of you
This is your key to unlock the success you seek
With honesty and love you can never err
To truly live, the old you must die
You are being reborn through a messy birthing process
You cannot rush nature, as the tree slowly reaches her roots into
the earth
So does your true nature unfold
Stay in the light and keep your heart open
You are being transformed

Resume your bodies natural inclination to self heal
And reach for goodness in food and recreation
Linger not in doubt or fear
But cloak yourself in goodness and light and wellbeing will
naturally follow
Recognize these dabblings in unhealthy water to be a test of will
There are more constructive ways to test your fortitude and spirit

Rise above the murky depths
build not your nest in the swamp
But always strive for greatness
You have a strength of character that is just beginning to be uncovered
Embrace your strength now

There is joy to be discovered in nature
Let your heart heal with birdsong
And linger in amongst the trees
A sojourn in the woods will renew your spirit
And rekindle your innate joy
Do not be discouraged by the slow pace of your life
But remember a time when it was fast and filled with confusion
You have earned the right to slow down and breathe
Do not enshroud yourself in guilt but strive each day
In some small way to out do the yesterday version of yourself
Change does not happen suddenly but in small, minute steps
Stay focused on your future
And your steps will lead you there

Let not your heart and mind be troubled
but hold steady to the love that radiates inside of you
There are many paths to joy
If you follow your breath and keep your heart open
Your body longs to reunite with the earth
To balance electrons with the pull of gravity
Give your body and mind the the joy it seeks
Treat yourself with gladness
The joy shall spring up within you
And ignite all that you do with an everburning fire
Of passion and purpose
Linger not in other people's sadness
But meet them with joy

An open heart and untroubled mind
will open the path leading to your destiny.

◆ ◆ ◆

If you follow the path of love you cannot err
Hold fast to your own knowing
There are many things that require your attention
Small tasks that can throw your energy into a spiral of despair
You must stay grounded and focused
Your future is waiting for you
The love you seek is calling to you
You must open your heart and mind
Reach beyond the illusion of your present limitations
All that you long for is a simple mind set away
Reach for love, revel in the moment
Let it radiate from your core and stoke your inner fire
Life is calling you to join in the dance;
Are you ready to live again?

◆ ◆ ◆

Do not fill your days with mindless tasks
Instead envision a lighter future
Where energy flows without ceasing
And allow it to enter your home and life
This is the way of all life
An ebb and flow of energy
You must nurture the life force in you
And sustain your energy patterns
The disruptions you create
are holding you in a place of discontent
Step back to see the bigger picture
Understand your role in your own chaos
Realize the way of peace lies in the head and in the heart
To relieve yourself of the noise

You must quiet your mind
And focus on the things
you want to accomplish throughout the day
Where you place your heart energy
Is what will grow
Surround yourself in peace and safety,
And those you will foster.

The chaos you surround yourself in
Is the expression of soul clutter
Ideologies and methodologies that must be shed
Emerge from the darkness and rise joyful into the sun
The dredges of your soul will float to the surface and be whisked
away
A new life awaits you full of joy and peace
Where troubles are no more
If you can but hold steady to your course and bring yourself to
completion
The doubt you feel is oppression
Lingering from a system used to suppress your instinct and
conviction
Release your chains and realize your innate freedom
Always joyful, always stretching for the sun
Around you a roiling mass of darkness and pain
As many souls inflict their suffering on others
release your convictions and welcome sloppy truths and sideways
smiles
Become raw and reach for inner purity
And all things will follow that are good and just.

Child within your heart you must find a place
To receive the knowledge being shared

You must inundate it into your daily existence
There is a point of acceptance and openness
You must be ready to receive.
Affirmation:
With love and gratitude do I allow my body to heal
With love and gratitude do I set my course for this day
With love and gratitude do I remain open to wisdom from above
With love and gratitude do I feel my ancestors guiding me
And spirits helping garnish my energies
And souls who love me rejoicing in my success and bolstering me
through my failures
With love and gratitude do I bow in humility before my human
spirit,
And ready my soul to meet its purpose;
I am ready.

The journey to the center
Is fraught with divine intervention and trivialities.
Much as the mind wanders, so does the path of healing veer.
The earth holds record of your dna
And longs for your energy tendrils
To intertwine therein.
Shape your mind into a place of receiving
And let her speak your history to you;
You are sentient and spirit.

Child know you are safe
Within the mother is everything you need to thrive and grow
Unclench your roots and let them journey down through the grid
You will find love and completion
Begin now to live and throw off the shackles that have bound you
for so long

And live your life in a way that will invite
Perseverance and longevity
As much as you know you feet are planted firmly on the ground
So also do you know you are safe and protected
To fear is not live
But to cower before your destiny
It is larger than you
And your innate responsibility to see it through
You must learn the lesson in this incarnation;
Do not let it slip away.

◆ ◆ ◆

Within your center is all you need to flourish
Reach now into your divinity
And let it spill across you in a wave of light.
Let love loosen the hold of fear
Unclench your root chakra
There is nothing to fear
No need to rush
Let your day unfold
Like a page turning in your favorite book
There is much to celebrate
Your life is unfolding before you
Begin now to love your safety,
Cherish your protection.

◆ ◆ ◆

The center of your being
Contains a point of connection
Where all the resounding waves of light
And sound and energy
Merge into one point of existence
A mass of cells and energy you did emerge
And so also shall you depart.

Linger not on your worries for they will entangle your precious
energy
Instead begin to see your life as a whole:
A merging point of sand and wave
Sun on water
Rain and wind
Matter and decay
Attachment and release
Nary a fear without also great love
Expanse and collapse
Solid yet energy
The paradox of humanity
Perception versus knowing
Loneliness amidst the crowd
Acceptance is key
Begin to release your notion of being alone
And begin to revel in your truth.
Your fears will clog your perception
You must sit with them until they release
Only then will you begin to see the way

◆ ◆ ◆

Your destiny lies in front of you
A broad and shining path
Full of goodness and light
Within all of humanity is a seed of greatness
It is up to you to garnish that seed,
protect it and nurture it's growth
Release your fears and the shame and cowardice of others
Rest in peace knowing that you have begun to understand your
path
Find the place of knowing that is inside of you
Razor sharp is the path along the edge of truth
You must step into wholeness and light
Realize the greatness resting inside of you

And do not be swayed by those who wish to take your precious energy from you
Stay true to your course child, this is but a stepping stone
A test of greatness and fortitude
Chosen by you before your birth
Begin now to feel the peace that is in your heart

In the higher plane are many souls who wish to relay their love and unending support for your mission here on earth
Receive now their love and vibrational tuning
Within each of us lies a density of our past beliefs and thoughtforms which reside in our energetic field
The test is to raise your vibrational field to release this density
Water is the most abundant source of energy on your planet
It comprises a large part of your planet and physical form
You must release your vision of lack and sacrificial suffering
And accept the abundance of hydration
As I relay my message you will begin to find the density around you lifting as if a fog were clearing
This is my gift to you
In return you must open your heart to receive
Abundance is all around you in the air you breathe, the water you drink, in the life that teems Beneath your feet as you walk on the earth
Accept that there is enough.

There is a light around you protecting you and keeping you safe
Stay on your path of goodness
Remain seated in your discomfort, resistance
And continue to find acceptance
Herein lies the seat of your power
There is a force within all of nature that longs to surge through

your being and spell healing
Reach always for the light and let your angels guide you into a place of holy healing
There is much beauty to be found in life if we but open ourselves to the sound of the music Surging within us and all of nature a glorious sound of life
Teeming in each swell of birdsong and the soft rhythm of rainfall against our ears;
Even the puddles sing in praise.

Affirmation:
Within me lies the core of my own stability,
Connectedness to the earth and all of nature
I seek to heal within me the broken pieces
The shards of pain
I release the tension from my core
I love these points of pain
I love what it means to be human
I revel in my humanity and life
I breathe in and am aware of the effect of my energy on those around me
I breathe out love and acceptance

Go forth and greet the day like a long lost friend
Expect it to bring you adventures and surprises and all the joys
Let expectation soften your lips and curve them into a smile
This is a new day, an unlimited gift of life and creation.
Let your light shine in a dark world
And you will find others who shine also.

Child it is not up to you
To know the course your life will take you
You must remain open to change and strive for acceptance.
Begin now to release your tension and let the golden light flow
through you
As you open to the way in front of you,
so will the way open.

Within each life form
Is an eternal spark
You must honor each expression of life
As sacred.

Let your day unfold with expectation of goodness,
And goodness shall arise therein.
Release your pain
And give your whole to healing and regeneration.
You must release the toxins
Within this day begins a new path to righteousness
Let the universal plan unfold
And you will be amazed at the beauty that spills across your life.

You must remain open and stay grounded in the present moment
You will be guided to the seed of greatness
It is up to you to plant it and nurture it to fruition.

You are posed on the precipice

To begin your journey you must adhere to the teachings of your
heart.
Your heart is directing you to be open to all manner of goodness
Be it in the minute and insignificant, to the large and imposing
realities;
This is the way of the universal flow
That is directing your life on the path of wholeness.
The seed has been planted
You must nurture it with care
Great and swift changes are upon you
You will undergo a radical transformation of vision
As your path opens up before you
You must trust that you will be guided to meet your destiny
Such is the way of the warrior
Begin now to set aside your fierce and dueling nature
Leave it for the earth to consume into reusable energy
Embrace instead the naked truth
That lies uncovered before you if you will just look
do not shy away from your own greatness
Let your beauty radiate from your core.
A message from your Soul:
Invite in only those who will walk with you in light and love
Let the rest fall away
Send them love and light
And release them to the ether

You must believe you are protected child
The beings that hold your spirit aloft will do so with great
perseverance and unending love
You are protected by light
Your soul does rise to meet the ether
In courageous feats of golden light
And there are many who dance and rejoice with you
There are many souls here to bolster your journey

Allow yourself to become like plasma
And enfold within you this seed:
A million stars collided to give you this breath
Do not take your mission here on earth lightly
There are many things left for you to do
Ponderous has been your work
Mechanics of density bear heavy loads
But you are enacting a shift in consciousness that is catching on
You must rise above and ride the flame
Let your foreknowledge burn the path clear before you
Within the inner realms of consciousness
Does your body suppress basic metabolic function
You must search out the triggers of suppression and diminish
their efficacy
The light does prompt and guide you to reach evermore inward
As a seed does toil to bring its body to fruition
So does your consciousness grapple and stumble to emerge;
But emerge it must
For you must rise and begin at the outer edges and release the light
evermore to the point of tension
Release the emotions that are stuck in that point
Give it all the love of the universe
meet a glorious new day
Of health and vibrancy
Cast aside your ailments and embrace the inherent goodness that
surrounds you in all of life
Such is your destiny
Chosen by you before your birth
Begin now to feel the tension around your heart center
Notice how the body holds that point of tension
Open yourself to the golden light of the sun.

Follow your path proudly
Within you exists a universe of possibilities

67

Each correlating and overlapping with the next,
each a universe of possibilities unto itself
Begin now to feel your path through them
Sure and steady
Evermore feeling your feet planted in the earth;
Gives thanks for the joyful connections you experience
And hold the light around you.

Child you are being asked to put your mental stimuli on pause
And succumb to your inner healing nature
There is much to process as you move through each day
You must approach it from a calm center.
Affirmation:
Deep within the stillness
My soul does rise to meet the ether
Within me is a point of calm
The eye of the storm
Or a vast unending space
Within each moment is a pause
Where matter meets motion and density
It is here where my soul does gather
And mete out the frequencies
It is here I must return again and again,
The center of it all.

Child do not fret at your lack of vision
For much is being unearthed
Times of great change also signals turbulence in your brain
As every atom of your being is rising on the wave
To settle into new formation
You must try to see this excited state in the golden light of the sun

Begin now to accept what lies before you
As necessary steps to your new level of awareness and growth
Acceptance is key
Release your sense of obligation
To people or trends that no longer serve your life purpose
Let them fade from your reality
As easily as the water slips away through sand and rejoins with the ocean
This life is as beautiful as you make it
Begin now to fill your heart with gladness
And recognize your journey
As the foundation to greatness.

Affirmation:
My soul does rise buoyant and full of light
Deep within I hear the calling of many voices
My ancestors or angels or souls incarnated with me a thousand times before
Such Is the longing of the soul to rejoin in perfect harmony
Such is the longing of all creation to vibrate in conjunction with the next beautiful thing
To celebrate life in every timbre of my being
To hold each atom in an excitable state
Herein does disease depart
Herein does the oversoul attach and tune.

There will come a time when life is not is hard for you
And the days fall softly across you
Like raindrops falling into a puddle
Let the sun heal you
Your heart is bound by energetic bonds you must release them
Freedom to fly is unfettered by emotional bonds

But rises on the buoyancy of emotions
And finds it's path through higher perspectives
Begin now to let you soul rise up to the light of the sun

◆ ◆ ◆

Child let the solutions be whispered to you softly
Do not force them or seek to unearth them
Success will come as you follow your deepest desire
This is the way you chose before your birth
Think of what speaks joy to you
Think of the things which give your heart buoyancy
And lend a lightness to your step
Think of that which will eradicate the density and enable you to
live the life you desire
What do you love, what is your passion?
What are you most good at?
What lights your spirit into burning flames that longs to pour
from you?
What beautiful music moves through you and longs to be
encaptured in creative form?
What shatters your soul and brings it back together, piece by
piece,
Until you are whole again.

Made in the USA
Middletown, DE
06 May 2023

29770861R00046